This journal belongs to:

____

____

EXPECTING YOU

A Keepsake Pregnancy Journal

TABLE OF CONTENTS

Hello, sweet one.

Right now, you are small—maybe only the size of a lentil or a plum. Soon, you'll be a tiny person snuggled in my arms, new to the world but long known to me.

As the years pass, you will learn to talk, how to put on your own pants, and how to follow your dreams. One day, you'll be able to read these words for yourself.

But for now, you are a part of me. Each day I spend expecting you brings new changes. Little by little, we're growing together.

This book is for both of us. It's a treasure chest of memories, stories, and feelings from this special time. It's a way for me to never forget the weeks and months leading up to what will be one of the biggest days of my life—your arrival.

This is the story of how you and I began.

YOUR BEGINNING

You started as an *idea*, a *hope*, and a *wish*.

YOUR BEGINNING

How I first found out you were coming:

Who I told:

How I felt:

What happened next:

My doctor or midwife is...

What I remember about my first appointments:

When I first heard your heartbeat, I...

I'm filled with plans and hopes about what's to come. My worries right now:

My wishes:

My cravings:

How life has changed already:

GROWING TOGETHER

Every week brings me *closer* to *you.*

Week ____________________

Dear little one,

Love, ____________________

Week ______________________

Dear little one,

Love, ______________________

Week ______________________________

Dear little one,

____

____

____

____

____

____

____

____

____

____

____

____

____

____

____

Love, ______________________________

Week ______________________

Dear little one,

Love, ______________________

Week ____________________

Dear little one,

Love, ____________________

Week ____________________

Dear little one,

Love, ____________________

Week ______________________________

Dear little one,

____

____

____

____

____

____

____

____

____

____

____

____

____

____

____

Love, ______________________________

Week ______________________

Dear little one,

____
____
____
____
____
____
____
____
____
____
____
____
____
____
____

Love, ______________________

Week ________________

Dear little one,

Love, ________________

Week ______________________________

Dear little one,

____

____

____

____

____

____

____

____

____

____

____

____

____

____

____

Love, ______________________________

Week ____________________

Dear little one,

Love, ____________________

Week ______________________

Dear little one,

____

____

____

____

____

____

____

____

____

____

____

____

____

____

____

Love, ______________________

Week ______________________

Dear little one,

____

____

____

____

____

____

____

____

____

____

____

____

____

____

____

Love, ______________________

Week ______________________

Dear little one,

Love, ______________________

Week ____________________

Dear little one,

Love, ____________________

Week ______________________________

Dear little one,

____

____

____

____

____

____

____

____

____

____

____

____

____

____

____

Love, ______________________________

Week ______________________

Dear little one,

____

____

____

____

____

____

____

____

____

____

____

____

____

____

____

Love, ______________________

Week ______________________________

Dear little one,

____

____

____

____

____

____

____

____

____

____

____

____

____

____

____

Love, ______________________________

Week ______________________

Dear little one,

Love, ______________________

Week ______________________

Dear little one,

____

____

____

____

____

____

____

____

____

____

____

____

____

____

____

Love, ______________________

Week ______________________________

Dear little one,

____

____

____

____

____

____

____

____

____

____

____

____

____

____

____

Love, ______________________________

Week ______________________

Dear little one,

____

____

____

____

____

____

____

____

____

____

____

____

____

____

____

Love, ______________________________

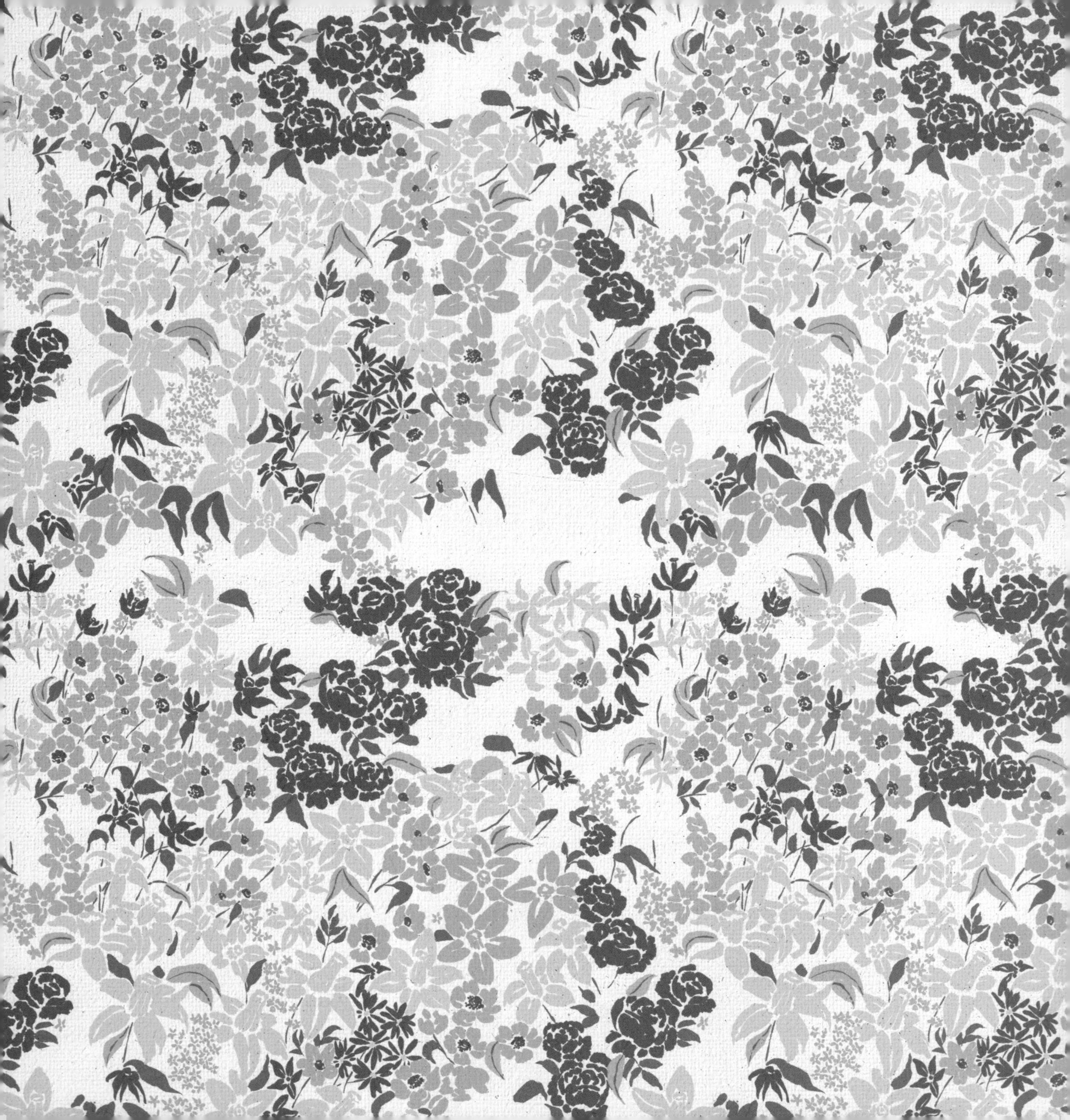

Week ______________________________

Dear little one,

____

____

____

____

____

____

____

____

____

____

____

____

____

____

____

Love, ______________________________

Week ______________________

Dear little one,

___

___

___

___

___

___

___

___

___

___

___

___

___

___

___

Love, ______________________

Week ______________________

Dear little one,

____

____

____

____

____

____

____

____

____

____

____

____

____

____

____

Love, ______________________

Week ______________________________

Dear little one,

____

____

____

____

____

____

____

____

____

____

____

____

____

____

____

Love, ______________________________

Week ____________________

Dear little one,

Love, ____________________

Week ______________________________

Dear little one,

Love, ____________________________

Week ______________________

Dear little one,

Love, ______________________

Week ______________________

Dear little one,

Love, ______________________

Week ______________________

Dear little one,

Love, ______________________

Week ______________________

Dear little one,

____

____

____

____

____

____

____

____

____

____

____

____

____

____

____

Love, ______________________________

Week ____________________

Dear little one,

Love, ____________________

Week ______________________________

Dear little one,

____
____
____
____
____
____
____
____
____
____
____
____
____
____
____

Love, ______________________________

Week ______________________

Dear little one,

____

____

____

____

____

____

____

____

____

____

____

____

____

____

____

Love, ______________________________

Week ______________________________

Dear little one,

____

____

____

____

____

____

____

____

____

____

____

____

____

____

____

Love, ______________________________

PREPARING FOR YOU

There's no *warmer nest* than the one you'll find in *my heart*.

YOUR BABY
SHOWER

We celebrated on ______________________ *at* ______________________________.
(date) (location)

The guest list:

Activities:

Memorable moments:

Some of the gifts you and I received:

NESTING

I've started to collect some things for you. These are a few of my favorites:

How I've designed your room or space:

How I picture us spending time at home together:

My favorite names for you (so far):

If ______________ was in charge, they'd name you ______________.

For now, I like to call you...

My Birth Plan

My Birth Plan

WAITING

Some of the ways I've been keeping busy:

Projects I hope to squeeze in before you're born:

Special things I'm doing for myself:

YOUR ARRIVAL

I thought I knew the dimensions of
life and *love*...until I held *you.*

INTRODUCING

____

(name)

Born on: ____________________ *at* ____________________

(day) *(time)*

Weight: ____________________________________

Length: ____________________________________

Head circumference: ____________________________

Your Birth Story

Your Birth Story

Your Birth Story

Your Birth Story

You'll *always*
be a part
of me.

An imprint of the Crown Publishing Group
A division of Penguin Random House LLC
1745 Broadway, New York, NY 10019
live-inspired.com | penguinrandomhouse.com

Copyright © 2026 by Compendium
Penguin Random House values and supports copyright. Copyright fuels creativity, encourages diverse voices, promotes free speech, and creates a vibrant culture. Thank you for buying an authorized edition of this book and for complying with copyright laws by not reproducing, scanning, or distributing any part of it in any form without permission. You are supporting writers and allowing Penguin Random House to continue to publish books for every reader. Please note that no part of this book may be used or reproduced in any manner for the purpose of training artificial intelligence technologies or systems.

Compendium and the Compendium colophon are registered trademarks of Penguin Random House LLC.

ISBN: 978-1-957891-73-6

Writer: Danielle Leduc McQueen
Designer: Chelsea Bianchini
Editor: Amelia Riedler
Production Manager: Olivia Holmes

1st printing. Manufactured in Malaysia with mineral oil–free inks on FSC®-Mix certified paper.

The authorized representative in the EU for product safety and compliance is Penguin Random House Ireland, Morrison Chambers, 32 Nassau Street, Dublin D02 YH68, Ireland, https://eu-contact.penguin.ie.

Create meaningful moments with gifts that inspire.

CONNECT WITH US
live-inspired.com | sayhello@compendiuminc.com

@compendiumliveinspired
#compendiumliveinspired